Wine Redefined

Wine Cocktails
Live a Little. Mix a Little.

Rebecca D. Kline
Life Passionista

wineredefined@gmail.com
wineredefined.com

Wine Cocktails Debut

Put down the etiquette and pick up a bottle~~it's time to be adventurous with wine. Treat your palate to a new experience filled with an "outside the bottle" approach to mixing cocktails.

Each "CockTale" presented in *"Mix it up"* shares a story of its origin intended to spark creativity and encourage a tale of your own.

No need to seek high and low, *"Jazz it up"* offers optional add-ons that can easily be found in your kitchen or local market to enhance your cocktail's appeal. For those seeking a little more flare, add the suggested spirit to *"Punch it up"*. Join me with your leftover wine, your extra juice from brunch and let's use what you've got.

For the wine snobs, be open-minded. It may surprise your palate, give you something trendy to talk about and even change your drinking personality. It may even make you more fun to be around. After all, wine does bring people together no matter how you drink it.

In this moment, be playful and let go of rules, pairings and formality. Wine Cocktails break the mold of traditional drink making and offer an experience to *Redefine Wine.*

Life is short. Live a little. Mix a little.

Table of Contents

Berry Black Night

Mix it up

2 ounces **Red Wine (Dry)**

2 ounces Blackberry Wine

1 ½ ounce Seltzer

2 drops Lime Juice

Jazz it up

Float Blackberries on top
or
Twist of Lime

Punch it up

½ ounce Gin

CockTale

How can one drink look so dark and ominous
but taste so good? That's exactly what you get with Berry
Black Night. It is fruity but not overpowering. You might have
to drink it during the day too!

Notes

Berry Creamsicle

Mix it up

2 ounces Rosé Wine (Sweet)

1 ounce Red Raspberry Wine (or other berry wine)

1 ounce Pomegranate Juice

½ ounce Pear Juice

½ ounce Half and Half

Punch it up

1 (750 ml) Rosé Wine (Sweet)

12 ounces Red Raspberry Wine

12 ounces Pomegranate Juice

6 ounces Pear Juice

6 ounces Half and Half

cockTale

This drink reminds you of a summertime Popsicle, but it's too good not to make year round!

Notes

Berry Good

Mix it up

4 ounces White Wine (Sparkling)

½ ounce Blackberry (or any berry) Syrup

Jazz it up

Float blueberries in glass

Hang orange slice on glass

cockTale

If you're looking to get more fruity, you've got to try this simple cocktail. Your favorite berry syrup combined with sparkling white wine will make you think - ooh it's so good!

Notes

Berry Peary

Mix it up

1 ½ ounce Berry Wine

2 ounces Rosé Wine

½ ounce Strawberry Daiquiri Mix 1 ounce Pear Juice

Jazz it up

Strain and serve with crushed ice
(or use blender to create a slushy)

Garnish with a Strawberry

Punch it up

Splash of white Rum or Tequila

Cocktale

Looking to get more fruit in your diet? Berry Peary might just be your answer and fun to boot. Sounds like it could be healthy too!

Notes

Blazing Hearth

Mix it up

4 ounces Red Wine (Dry, peppery adds flare)

2 ounces Cranberry Juice

½ tablespoon Agave Nectar

Jazz it up

Garnish with Cinnamon Sticks

Punch it up

Splash of Cinnamon Liqueur or Cinnamon Whiskey
Optional: Mull ingredients and serve warm

cockTale

This drink puts you in the mood to cuddle up beside a blazing fireplace on a cold night. The taste of cranberry and cinnamon set the tone for a cozy time.

Notes

Blue - Pom

Mix it up

1 ½ ounce Blueberry Wine

1 ½ ounce Pomegranate Wine

1 ½ ounce **White Wine (Dry)**

½ ounce Pomegranate Juice

Splash of Lemon Lime Seltzer

Jazz it up

Garnish with slices of Star Fruit

cockTale

Fruity but not too sweet; that's perfect on the palate.
The dry white provides the right finishing touch.

Notes

Blue Resolution

Mix it up

5 ounces White Wine (Sparkling)

1 ounce Blueberry Juice

Jazz it up

Rim glass with sugar
Garnish with twist of lime

Punch it up

Splash of Gin & a touch of lime

cockTale

One taste of this drink and you will resolve to
drink it again and again. Just be careful, it
does have a little kick to it!

Notes

Blue Surprise

Mix it up

3 ounces White Wine (Sweet)

1 ½ ounce Blue Sports Drink

¾ ounce Ginger Beer

½ ounce Seltzer

Jazz it up

Serve in a fun glass to show off the color.

cockTale

This unique combination will be smooth to your pallet. Sweet, tart and spicy are all tastes you will experience. Truly a surprise!

Notes

Blueberry Bobble

Mix it up

1 ½ ounce Rosé Wine (Sweet)

1 ½ ounce Blueberry Wine

1 ounce Blueberry Juice

Jazz it up

Garnish with a Strawberry

Punch it up

Gin to taste

cockTale

If you like blueberries, this drink is for you. You will love this cocktail so much you will bobble your head nodding in approval of this wonderful nectar of the berry. You may not want to bobble in public!

Notes

Caddy Cats

Mix it up

3 ounces White Wine (Sweet or Sparkling)

1 ounce Rosé Wine (Sweet)

1 ounce Pomegranate Juice

Jazz it up

Serve on the rocks

Punch it up

1 (750 ml) Rosé Wine (Sweet)

1 (750 ml) White Wine (Sweet or Sparkling Wine)

4 Cups Pomegranate Juice

CockTale

Don't be caught in the alley drinking "Caddy Cats." You never know who you will meet. The Pomegranate Juice brings out the unique blend of these two "catty" wines.

Notes

Cherry Dolce

Mix it up

1 ½ ounce White Wine (Sparkling)

1 ounce Red Wine (Sweet)

1 ounce White Wine (Sweet)

½ teaspoon Agave Nectar

Jazz it up

Rim with Sugar

cocktale

As the name suggests, this is a drink
created for sweet cherry lovers. Don't be
fooled, the cherries must be invisible because
the flavor jumps on your palate.

Notes

Cherry Tart

Mix it up

2 ½ ounces White Wine (Dry)

1 ½ ounce Cherry Wine

1 ounce Red Wine (Dry)

1 ounce Cherry Juice

Jazz it up

Rim with Sugar

Garnish with a Drunken Cherry

cockTale

Like a tart hot out of the oven, this unique
combination will be pleasant on your palate.
Don't let the taste fool you. It's been called
a cherry bomb.

Notes

Cherryola

Mix it up
4 ounces Cherry wine

1 ounce favorite cola

Jazz it up
Garnish with a cherry

Punch it up
Rum to taste

COCKTALE

Sometimes there's nothing like a good old fashion soda. Just add the wine, relax, and call an old friend.

Notes

Colada Cat

Mix it up

4 ounces Red Wine (Sweet)

1 ounce Pear Juice

1 ounce Piña Colada Mix

Jazz it up

Rim glass first with honey & coconut

cockTale

This is a Piña Colada wanna be. However, after tasting this cat you'll be glad it's a colada cat. Meow!

Notes

Dark Sparkle

Mix it up

2 ½ ounces Red Wine (Dry)

2 ½ ounces White Wine (Sparkling)

Jazz it up

Rim with sugar

Punch it up

Splash of Blackberry Vodka

Cocktale

Think of someone with dark brown eyes
with a secret they want to tell. This drink is
like those eyes sparkling back at you –
exciting yet mysterious. Try this drink and
feel the excitement!

Notes

Evening Breeze

Mix it up

3 ounces Red Wine (Dry)

2 ounces Ginger Beer

Jazz it up

Garnish with cinnamon stick

Punch it up

½ ounce Spiced Rum

Cocktale

Like an evening breeze, this cocktail speaks
of things to come. When feeling a chilly night
approaching, the cozy fire is waiting.

Notes

French Kiss

Mix it up

2 ounces Rosé Wine

1 ounce Red Wine (Sweet)

1 ounce White Wine (Sweet)

Jazz it up

Rim with cinnamon and sugar

cockTale

French Kiss starts with Sweet White and
Sweet Red to create the sweetness of the
kiss. It finishes with Rose´ for that blush you
experience after the kiss. Be prepared, this
kiss is strong.

Notes

From the Garden

Mix it up

6 ounces White Wine (Sweet)

5 drops Lavender Bitter OR 1 drop of Lavender Essential Oil

Jazz it up

Garnish with Star Fruit and/or Spearmint Leaves

cockTale

This cocktail takes you straight to the garden as the aroma of lavender rises from the glass and the taste mingles with the sweet fruit of summer.

Notes

Fruit Salad

Mix it up

2½ ounces Red Wine (Sweet)

1 ounce Pomegranate Juice/ Cranberry Juice

1 ounce Mango Juice/ Pineapple Juice

Jazz it up

Garnish with pineapple and rim with cinnamon

Punch it up

Vodka to taste

cockTale

It is easy to see from the ingredients why this cocktail is called fruit salad. Just be careful because you will want to drink it too fast. With all of the fruit juice, it must be healthy too.

Notes

Heat Wave

Mix it up

5 ounces Hard Cider - Chilled

½ teaspoon Hot Sauce – Room Temperature

Jazz it up

Serve in a Highball Glass

Cocktale

This drink makes you think of that first glass of fall cider in a whole new way. Even though the drink is cold, you will be warmed from the inside out while sipping this sizzling cider.

Notes

How Sweet It Is

Mix it up

1 ½ ounce Rosé Wine (Sweet)

1 ½ ounce White Wine (Sweet)

1 ounce Sweet Green Tea

½ ounce Tonic Water

Jazz it up

Garnish with Star fruit Slice

Muddle Mint Leaves

Punch it up

Splash of Triple Sec

cockTale

This drink lives up to its name. The green tea and tonic water create a flavor you won't soon forget.

Notes

In A Hurry

Mix it up

2 ounces Apple Wine
1 ounce Rosé Wine (Sweet)
1 ½ ounce Cranberry/Pomegranate Juice
½ ounce Orange Juice
½ tablespoon Simple Syrup (or less to taste)
Splash Lime Juice

Jazz it up

Garnish with an Orange Slice on the rim

Punch it up

18 ounces Cranberry Juice/ Pomegranate Juice
6 ounces Orange Juice
1½ ounces Lime Juice
6 tablespoons Simple Syrup (less to taste)
12 ounces Rosé Wine (Sweet)

CockTale

Even though this cocktail is called "In A Hurry", you're going to want to take your time drinking it. It is sure to be a sensation with this combination of fruit juices and wines. Take your time and enjoy!

Notes

In Like a Lion

Mix it up

2 ounce Rosé Wine (Dry)

2 ounces White Wine (Sweet)

½ ounce Coffee

Agave to taste

Jazz it up

Garnish with one whole Coffee Bean

Punch it up

Splash of Coffee Liqueur

Cocktale

Just as March roars onto the scene like a lion this drink will grab your attention with a hint of coffee and, of course, a little caffeine too!

Notes

Lively Lime

Mix it up

5 ounces White Wine (Sparkling)

1 ½ ounce Lime Juice

¼ teaspoon Simple Syrup

Jazz it up

For fun sink 2 pieces of Green Rock Candy

Rim glass with sugar

Punch it up

Splash of Gin

cockTaLe

Dry wine lovers can skip the simple syrup
and give this drink a whirl. You may surprise
yourself! You may even become lively!

Notes

Mango Fizz

Mix it up

3 ounces White Wine (Sparkling)

1 ½ ounce Orange Wine

1 ounce Mango Nectar

Jazz it up

Garnish with Mango slice

Punch it up

Gin to taste

8 ounces Mango Nectar

12 ounces Orange Wine

1 (750 ml) White Wine (Sparkling)

COCKTALE

Take a trip to the tropics and never leave the comfort of your own home. Orange and Mango are a natural combination. The sparkling wine gives it just the right touch.

Notes

Mangomosa

Mix it up

4 ounces White Wine (Sparkling)

3 ounces White Wine (Sweet)

2 ounces Mango/Pineapple Juice

Jazz it up

Garnish with Mango or Pineapple

Punch it up

24 ounces Mango Juice/Pineapple Juice

2 bottles (750 ml x 2) White Wine (Sparkling)

Cocktale

This is a quick and easy drink to mix up for brunch, lunch or dinner. It will go down smooth. You will forget how many times you've filled your glass until the bottles are empty.

Notes

Mango Tango

Mix it up

2 ounces White Wine (Dry)

2 ounces White Wine (Sparkling)

2 ounces Mango Nectar

Jazz it up

Garnish with Mango Slice

Punch it up

Vodka to taste

2 (750 ml x 2) White Wine (Dry)

1 (750 ml) White Wine (Sparkling)

4 cups Mango Nectar

Cocktale

One glass of this exciting drink and you will feel like dancing the Tango. What a great combination of nectar and wine!

Notes

Merblu

Mix it up

3 ounces Blueberry Wine

2 ounces Merlot

Jazz it up

Float Blueberries in glass
(frozen is nice in summer)

Cocktale

This simple and easy to make cocktail is a fun variation from your normal evening glass of wine. Change it up a little and try it!

Notes

Night and Day

Mix it up

2 ounces White Wine (Sweet)

2 ounces Red Wine (Dry)

1 ounce Pomegranate Juice

Jazz it up

Float Black Raspberries on top

CockTale

The dark wines and the light wines create
the perfect of opposites. A beautiful dry
finish softened by the fruity berries floating
on top.

Notes

Orange Berry Twist

Mix it up

1 ½ ounce Red Raspberry Wine

1 ounce White Wine (Sparkling)

3 ½ ounces Orange Juice

Jazz it up

Garnish with Orange Slice

CockTale

This is a simple twist on a traditional mimosa.

No sparkles but lots of vitamin C.

Notes

Orange Burst

Mix it up

2 ounces White Wine (Sweet)

2 ounces Orange Wine

2 ounces White Wine (Sparkling)

Jazz it up

Garnish with a floating Mandarin Orange Section

Punch it up

1 (750 ml) White Wine (Sweet)

1 (750 ml) Orange Wine

½ bottle White Wine (Sparkling)

Cocktale

Wish you were in Florida? Orange Burst will make you think you are right in the middle of an Orange Grove. Go on vacation without ever leaving the comfort of your home.

Notes

Peach Cobbler

Mix it up

2 ounces White Wine (Dry)

½ ounce Rosé Wine

2 ½ ounces Peach Bellini

½ teaspoon Lime Juice

Jazz it up

Garnish with Peach

Rim glass with Honey

Punch it up

For the daring...add Honey Moonshine to taste

Cocktale

One sniff of this cocktail and you'll think you
are in Grandma's kitchen as the peach
cobbler comes out of the oven. Wait until you
taste it, you will want that cobbler to pair
with it.

Notes

Peachy Keen

Mix it up

1 ounce White Wine (Dry)

1 ½ ounce White Wine (Sparkling)

2 ½ ounces Peach Bellini or Peach Juice (or Peach Wine for

an extra kick)

Jazz it up

Serve on the rocks

Punch it up

Splash of Gin

1 (750 ml) White Wine (Dry)

1 (750 ml) White Wine (Sweet)

18 ounces Peach Bellini or Peach juice

Add Ice Cubes, Peaches and Mint

CockTale

Sipping this drink takes you straight to the peach orchard. The mingling of the wines and Peach Bellini or juice gives just the right flavor to this fruity treat.

Notes

Pear with Me

Mix it up

2 ounces White Wine (Sparkling)

1 ounce Orange Wine or Peach Wine

2 ½ ounces Pear Juice

Jazz it up

Rim with orange slice

CockTale

This is a drink you have to have with brunch or on a warm summer's evening. It is light yet full of fruity richness. You may even want to drink it anytime of the year to remind you of the sun.

Notes

Pearly Sweet

Mix it up

2 ½ ounces Apple Wine

2 ounces Sweet Green Tea

1 ounce Pear Juice

Jazz it up

Float a mint leaf to garnish

CockTale

Pearly Sweet could possibly be the next health craze. You get the nutrition of pear juice and sweet green tea, along with the calming effect of the Apple Wine. "To your Health"!

Notes

Pineapple Whisper

Mix it up

3 ounces White Wine (Dry)

1 ounce Pineapple Juice

1 ounce Ginger Beer

Jazz it up

Garnish with Pineapple slice

CockTale

White Wine with Ginger Beer and Pineapple
Juice- really? Try it. The ginger helps the
flavors to stand out and the pineapple comes
across as a whisper in your mouth

Notes

Pom-Pom

Mix it up

2 ounces Red Wine (Sweet)

1 ounce Pomegranate or Blackberry Wine

1 ounce Rosé Wine (Sweet)

1 ounce Pomegranate Juice

Jazz it up

Garnish with Blackberry on Rim

Punch it up

½ ounce Pomegranate Liqueur for depth

cockTale

We're not talking cheerleaders,
but if you like pomegranate you
will be cheering for this drink!

Notes

Red Delicious

Mix it up

2 ½ ounces Red Wine (Sweet)

2 ½ ounces Apple Wine

Jazz it up

Rim with Hot Chocolate Powder

Punch it up

1 (750ml) Apple Wine

1 (750ml) Red Wine (Sweet)

1 Liter Seltzer Water

Float apples on top

CockTale

A sip of this Red Delicious is like biting into a sweet juicy red apple. Once you start you can't stop until it's gone!

Notes

Red Dimples

Mix it up

3 ounces Red Wine (Dry)

2 ounces Orange Juice

Shake it up

Jazz it up

Rim glass with sugar or fresh citrus

Punch it up

Tequila to taste
or
1 drop of citrus essential oil

Cocktale

Try Orange Wine instead of Orange Juice to add some spunk to this cocktail. This combination with the red wine, will bring out the dimples on your cheeks.

Notes

Rendezvous Adventure

Mix it up

2 ounces White Wine (Sparkling)

1½ ounces Rosé Wine (Dry)

1 ounce Red Wine (Sweet)

1 ounce Blueberry Juice

Jazz it up

Float Blueberries in glass

Punch it up

Vodka to taste

Cocktale

This unique combination of flavors is just like the many feelings you get when a rendezvous is planned with a special someone. Find that person and enjoy this cocktail.

Notes

Rosey Cheeks

Mix it up

4 ounces White Wine (Sparkling)

1 ounce Mango Juice

1 ounce Cranberry Juice

Jazz it up

Garnish with Mango slice on glass

Punch it up

12 ounces Mango Juice

12 ounces Cranberry Juice

2 bottles White Wine (Sparkling)

CockTale

If you're an outdoors person you probably already have "Rosey Cheeks". Rather than spending a day in the sun and wind, try this cocktail. The cranberry mango combination will give you that glow.

Notes

Scarlet Rose

Mix it up

2 ½ ounces Merlot

2 ½ ounces Rosé Wine (Sweet)

Jazz it up

Garnish with Strawberry

Rim with Cinnamon and Sugar

Punch it up

Cinnamon Liqueur to taste

1 (750 ml) Merlot

1 (750 ml) Rosé Wine (Sweet)

COCKTALE

If you are into reds, you will "give a damn" about this scarlet! Just be careful. You may be three sheets to the wind but it's better than "Gone with the Wind".

Notes

Sparkling Cherry

Mix it up

4 ounces White Wine (Sparkling)

2 ounce Cherry Wine

Jazz it up

Serve in Champagne Flute

Rim glass with sugar

Punch it up

1 (750 ml) White Wine (Sparkling)

12 ounces Cherry Wine

CockTale

This is a great alternate to traditional sparkling wines. It adds that unique cherry flavor for a toast to warmer weather!

Notes

Spice It Up

Mix it up

3 ounces White Wine (Sparkling)

2 ounces Red Wine (Sweet)

1 ounce Cranberry Juice

Jazz it up

Cinnamon Hearts to taste

Punch it up

Cinnamon Liqueur to taste

1 (750 ml) Red Wine (Sweet)

2 (750 ml x 2) White Wine (Sparkling)

32 ounces Cranberry Juice

93

CockTale

Spice it up combines a variety of flavors into one drink. The sweet wines mingle with the tartness of the cranberry juice and the cinnamon hearts add just the right amount of spice.

Notes

Star Gazer

Mix it up

2 ounces White Wine (Sparkling)

1 ounce White Wine (Dry)

1 ounce Red Wine (Dry)

Jazz it up

Rim glass with sugar and cinnamon

Cocktale

This cocktail is the perfect companion for sitting out on your favorite chaise and looking up at the stars. It will put you in that mellow mood to sit and gaze at the cosmos. Don't forget to make a second drink for the person who joins you!

Notes

Strawberry Patch

Mix it up

2 ounces White Wine (Sparkling)

2 ounces Rosé Wine

1 ounce Strawberry Daiquiri Mix

Jazz it up

Garnish with Fresh Strawberries

CockTale

If you close your eyes while tasting this drink
you will think you are right there in the
strawberry patch eating fresh strawberries.
Open your eyes, you may miss the person
wanting to join you for a drink!

Notes

Sun Kissed

Mix it up

4 ounces Orange Wine or Peach Wine

2 ounces Seltzer Water

1 drop Lime Juice

1 drop Lemon Juice

Jazz it up

Garnish with lime or lemon slice and rim with sugar

Punch it up

Splash of Mango Rum

COCKTALE

This drink will take you to the tropics. You will feel the kiss of the sun as this luscious mix of fruity flavors hits your palate.

Notes

Sunrise

Mix it up

4 ounces Rosé Wine (Sweet)

2 tablespoons Mango Puree

2 ounces Tonic Water

Jazz it up

Add frozen Mango slices

Punch it up

White Rum to taste

2 (750 ml x 2) Rosé Wine (Sweet)

1 ½ cups Mango Puree

24 ounces Tonic Water

CockTale

This could be the new "Mimosa." The
sweetness of the mango and the zest of the
Rosé with the fizz of the tonic water will
start anyone's day off on the right foot or
add to the enjoyment of their evening!

Notes

Sweet Blush

Mix it up

1 ounce Rosé Wine (Sweet)

1 ounce White Wine (Sweet)

1 ounce Orange Mango Red Tea

Simple Syrup or Agave Nectar to taste

Jazz it up

Garnish with a floating Mandarin Orange section

Punch it up

Gin to taste

1 (750 ml) Rosé Wine (Sweet)

1 (750 ml) White Wine (Sweet)

4 cups Orange Mango Red Tea

1 cup Simple Syrup

CockTale

Drink this slowly. Let the sweetness fill you.
Soon you'll feel the blush on your cheeks just
like that first date or maybe even that first
kiss!

Notes

Sweet Stuff

Mix it up

6 ounces White Wine (Sparkling)

¼ Teaspoon Vanilla

½ Teaspoon Lemon Juice

Simple Syrup to taste

Jazz it up

Garnish with Lemon slice

Punch it up

Gin to taste

CockTale

Vanilla and Lemon - who'd have thought they'd go so well together. Mixed with the sparkling wine those two create the perfect blend.

Notes

Sweet Tart

Mix it up

2 ½ ounces Rosé Wine (Sweet)

1 ounce Red Wine (Sweet)

1 ½ ounce Tonic Water

Jazz it up

Garnish with Lime or Lemon

CockTale

Sweet Tart is just a little tart. It may remind you of one of your favorite candies growing up. Not your normal cocktail.

Notes

Tea in Hiding

Mix it up

2 ½ ounces White Wine (Sparkling)

2 ½ ounces Sweet Green Tea

Jazz it up

Garnish with Star Fruit Slice

Add fresh mint

Add one drop Mint Essential Oil

Cocktale

This is an amazing combination blending the
smooth flavor of green tea with the fun of a
sparkling wine.
This may be a medicinal drink!

Notes

Twisted Apple

Mix it up

2 ounces Apple Wine

2 ounces Raspberry Wine

1 ½ ounce Blackberry Juice

Jazz it up

Garnish with Orange slice

Punch it up

Cinnamon Whiskey to taste

cockTale

Oh yes - this is a twisted fruity drink. The orange and raspberry wines play well together. The cranberry/tangerine juice puts the perfect finish to this twisted drink

Notes

Warm Apple Pie

Mix it up

2 ounces Apple Wine

¼ Teaspoon Real Vanilla

4 ounces Hot Hard Cider

Jazz it up

Top with Whipped Cream and Cinnamon
or
Rim glass with cinnamon

Cocktale

Imagine sniffing the apple pie just as it's coming out of the oven. All your senses will experience this "just baked" cocktail.

Notes

White Ginger

Mix it up

3 ounces White Wine (Dry)

2 ounces Ginger Beer

Jazz it up

Twist of lime on the rim

Punch it up

Spiced Rum to taste

CockTale

Ginger adds a special touch to the dryness of the white wine. Its unique sensation on your palate will make you want more.

Notes

Winey Rabbit

Mix it up

1 ounce White Wine (Sweet)

1 ounce White Wine (Dry)

1 ½ ounce Carrot Juice

1 ½ ounce Pear Juice

Jazz it up

Serve in a lowboy glass and act like a grown-up

cockTale

Rabbits know the value of a carrot. But people can be crazy, who would add carrot juice to wine? Stop being a winey rabbit and try it!

Notes

Index

wineredefined.com

wineredefined@gmail.com

63410556R00068

Made in the USA
Charleston, SC
02 November 2016